Life of the Prophet Muhammad

1st Edition

(1419 AH/1998 AC)

The Life of the Prophet Muhammad

A Brief History
by
M. M. Pickthall

Introduction by
Khalid Yahya Blankinship

amana publications
Beltsville, Maryland USA

© Copyrights 1419 AH/1998 AC by
amana publications
10710 Tucker Street Suite B
Beltsville, Maryland 20705-2223 USA
Tel: (301) 595-5777
Fax: (301) 595-5888
WWW.amana-publications.com
Email: igamana@erols.com

Library of Congress catologing-in-publications Data

Pickthall, Marmaduke William, 1875–1936.
    The life of the prophet Muhammad : a brief history / by
M. M. Pickthall : introduction by Khalid Yahya Blankinship.
      p. cm.
    ISBN 0–915957–86–8
    1. Muḥammad, Prophet, d. 632. 2. Muslims--Saudi
Arabia--Biography. I. Title.
BP75.P48 1998
297.6'3--dc21   ·
[B]   98–35847
                                  CIP

Printed in the United States of America by
International Graphics
10710 Tucker Street
Beltsville, Maryland 20705-2223 USA
Tel: (301) 595-5999
Email: igfx@aol.com

CONTENTS

INTRODUCTION

Muhammad Marmaduke Pickthall (1292–1355/ 1875–1936) was an outstanding English Muslim pioneer and man of letters. Born into a family of Anglican clergymen, he grew up having a sensitive and romantic nature which, as a young man living at the very pinnacle of British imperialist domination, led him to the Muslim world. Today, we can only try to imagine how hard it must have been for an Englishman of that time to escape from the effects of racism inculcated by British tradition, training, and power. Not surprisingly, Pickthall began with the usual inclination of the Victorian British to support their own country's imperial policies. This was in line with Pickthall's family tradition of support for the Tory party, the party of the arch-imperialist Disraeli. Yet Pickthall's facility with languages, his sympathetic nature, and the sense of warmth he derived from being with the common people drew him away from his own countrymen and toward the Muslims. Even during his early visits to Arabic-speaking countries (1311–1313/1894–1896, 1325/1907, 1326–1327/1908– 1909), during which he quickly learnt Arabic, he expressed a sympathy for the Muslim inhabitants and their viewpoint that was exceptional for a Victorian Englishman. He was impressed by the social solidarity and togetherness of the Muslims he met, their happiness with the simple life, their lack of materialistic grasping, and their fine hospitality, charity, and kindness.

Building on his experiences in the Muslim countries, he began his career as a writer, a career that burgeoned from 1315/1898 on. He began to produce novels, scoring a striking success with *Said the Fisherman* in 1321/1903, a work which won the praise of such eminent writers as James Barrie, H. G. Wells, and D. H. Lawrence. He produced fourteen novels in all between 1317/1900 and 1339/1921, as well as numerous short stories. Had he wanted to remain simply a successful novelist, lionized by English-speaking natives, he could easily have done so. But he also gradually acquired an ideological dimension, represented in his many journalistic pieces on the politics of the Muslim world, including polemical ones about European intervention and aggression. He undertook such writing because, in contrast to the callous imperialists, he cared about the Muslim people who had treated him so kindly.

Thus it was that he was drawn away from support of the British empire and toward Islam, as he gradually developed a sympathy for the Ottoman Turkish empire as the protagonist of universalist and progressive Islam. This trend was already apparent in 1325/1907, when he favored increasing the Ottomans' role in British-occupied Egypt. During the Balkan Wars against Turkey (1330–1331/1912–1913), Pickthall became a strong partisan of the Turks. He even visited Istanbul for four months in 1331/1913, during which time he met various important Turkish leaders, including the minister of interior, Tal'at Pasha, and the Islamizing

2

future prime minister, Sa'id Halim Pasha. On returning, he helped to found the Anglo-Ottoman Society in 1332/1914, but this endeavor was soon overtaken by the catastrophe of the First World War, which brought his own Britain to war with his beloved Turkey for a long period (1332–1337/1914–1918).

This fateful development led to the severest crisis of Pickthall's life: the dilemma of whether to support the cause of his country or of justice as he saw it. He clearly chose the latter, categorically refusing to fight against Turkey and instead writing in its support to politicians and in newspapers, even though it was now an enemy of Britain. As a result, Pickthall's linguistic and other skills were not in demand in the war with the British government, which instead treated him disdainfully and insultingly.[1] But Pickthall's dilemma also went beyond politics to the spiritual realm, pushing him over the boundary from Christianity into Islam as his personal religion.

As a religious person who had been a practicing Christian all his life, Pickthall had nevertheless long contemplated embracing Islam. As early as about 1312/1894, he told the *Shaykh al 'Ulamā'* of the Umayyad Mosque in Damascus of his wish to embrace Islam, but the shaykh dissuaded him, saying he was too young.[2] Later, in Istanbul in 1331/1916, he told Tal'at Pasha, the Turkish interior minister, that he intended to embrace Islam, but Tal'at persuaded

---

1. Anne Fremantle, *Loyal Enemy* (London: Hutchinson & Co., 1938), pp. 271–273, 275–276.

2. Fremantle, *Loyal Enemy,* pp. 81–82; Peter Clark, *Marmaduke Pickthall: British Muslim*, (London: Quartet Books, 1986), p. 37.

him to wait until he returned to England to take that step.[3] Once back to England, Pickthall continued to attend church and practice Anglican Christianity, until later in that same year when an anti-Muslim sermon and hymn so offended him that he left the church and never went back.[4] Left in a spiritual vacuum, he entered Islam in al Muharram 1333/December 1914, finding solace and reassurance in the Qur'an.[5] However, he did not seek a more public role in the religion until he began his association with the Woking mosque near London in 1336/1917.[6] After that, he regularly gave lectures, delivered sermons, and led worship there and at another mosque in London, preaching in Arabic as well as English and even attaining to the position of imam.

As a result of his changed attitude and his hardened position against Britain's foreign policy, Pickthall could not find suitable work in England and ended up in India working for Muslims, first as the editor of an anti-colonial newspaper in Bombay (1339–1343/1920–1924). During this period, he was associated with Muhammad 'Ali, the leader of the *Khilafat* movement, and with Gandhi. In 1343–1353/1925–1935, he found his final, longest, and best

---

3. Arafat K. El-Ashi, *Why We Embraced Islam,* (Kuwait: Scientific Research House, 1977, 1980), vol. V, pp. 61–62.

4. Fremantle, *Loyal Enemy,* p. 227.

5. Muriel Pickthall, "A Great English Muslim," *Islamic Culture,* XI (1937):138–142; Fremantle, *Loyal Enemy,* p. 252; El-Ashi, *Why We Embraced Islam,* vol. V, p. 62. Thus, Pickthall practiced Islam for over twenty-one years of his life.

6. Fremantle, *Loyal Enemy,* p. 296. It appears that the claim in Clark's *Marmaduke Pickthall: British Muslim* on pages 38 and 42, that it was only at this time that he embraced Islam at all, is incorrect. Perhaps he made a second, more publicized avowal of his having become a Muslim in 1336/1917.

employment as a scholar under the Nizam of Hyderabad, who was the ruler of the largest Muslim state at that time. In Hyderabad, he started in 1345/1927 and edited *Islamic Culture,* a scholarly journal that still appears today. This journal, which he established with the highest academic standards, immediately became a major medium of scholarship on Islam in English. In 1354/1935, shortly before his death, he returned to England.

Muhammad Pickthall is deserving of recognition for his exceptional courage and perseverance as an early English Muslim. Out of thousands of English gentlemen of his generation, when British imperialism was at its height, almost alone he chose to embrace Islam. He became a Muslim in spite of the fact that at first he too tended to view the Muslims, in a tension of "us" versus "them," as people who needed to be tutored by the English. But his humane nature, which could not abide the oppression and hypocrisy he saw, led him to favor the civilizing force of Islam, even though his choice meant being ostracized by his own people, and even though he faced unemployment as a result of his persistence. Though Muriel—his wife for almost forty years—stood by him, even embracing Islam herself in 1340/1922, the social isolation the couple faced was a strain, perhaps compounded by their having no children. Through all, Pickthall remained unswervingly loyal to Islam and to the Muslims among whom he found himself, the bonds of faith replacing those of blood. Pickthall really practiced Islam both in its ethics and its rituals, observing both the five daily *salat*s and the fast of Ramadan. He also memorized a considerable part of the Qur'an.[7] Inspired by his memory, sev-

---

7.   Clark, *Marmaduke Pickthall: British Muslim,* p. 62.

eral former students of his from Hyderabad hotly defended him, his sincerity, and his Arabic erudition when these were called into question in 1402/1982 by a Pakistani.[8]

Pickthall's main life work was his translation of the Qur'an, which he began about 1336/1918 and was able to carry to completion mainly because of the Nizam's patronage. Chronologically, it is the tenth complete translation in English. In it, Pickthall used old-fashion English and stuck to a fairly literal translation as had most of his predecessors. Nevertheless, Pickthall's style is often very eloquent and his translation more accurate than others. Pickthall is clearly somewhat dependent on the earlier translation of the Ahmadi Muhammad 'Ali of Lahore, the first edition of which appeared in 1335/1917, as well as those of Palmer and Rodwell. In a way, Pickthall's work is a revision of these other works from a mainstream Sunni point of view. Indeed, during his visit to Egypt in 1348/1929–1930, Pickthall revised his work and with the help of the Egyptian professor Muhammad Ahmad al Ghamrawi, consulted the Shaykh of al Azhar, Mustafa al Maraghi, on controversial points. During this time he also received the support of Muhammad Rashid Rida. Since its first publication in 1349/1930, Pickthall's translation has been continually in print and has literally circled the globe, becoming one of the most widely-used of all translations.

Among the most attractive aspects of Pickthall's translation are his own contributions: his helpful explanatory and historical notes on the *surah*s and his excellent introduction, which gives a biography of the Prophet Muhammad's life.

---

8. Ibid., p. 67.

This brief biography, which is reproduced here,[*] is truly a gem of concision, containing all that is most essential about the mission of the Prophet. It presents a complete and sympathetic picture in a startlingly small space. At the same time, Pickthall's presentation is realistic and nonapologetic. Because of its brevity, this biography remains eminently suitable as an introduction to the Prophet's life for those wanting a quick look based on the earliest and most authentic Muslim sources. It truly represents what Muslims immediately recall when they think about the history of the Prophet Muhammad, may Allah bless him and grant him peace.

Khalid Yahya Blankinship
Temple University
Rabi' al Awwal 1419 A.H.
June 1998 A.C.

---

[*] The original has been expanded to include the Qur'an referenced by the author and its English translation [Editor's note].

AT MAKKAH

MUHAMMAD, son of 'Abd Allāh, son of 'Abd al Muṭṭalib, of the tribe of Quraysh, was born in Makkah fifty-three years before the Hijrah. As his father died before he was born, the young Muhammad was raised under the protection of his grandfather 'Abd al Muṭṭalib and, after this man's death, by his uncle Abū Ṭālib. As a young boy, he travelled with his uncle in the merchants' caravan to Syria and, some years later, made the same journey in the service of a wealthy widow named Khadījah. So faithfully did he transact her business and so excellent was the report of his behavior that she received from her old servant who had accompanied him, that she soon proposed to and then married her young agent. The marriage proved to be a very happy one, though she was (reported to be) fifteen years older than he was. Throughout the twenty-six years of their life together, Muhammad was devoted to her. Even after her death, when he married other women, he always mentioned her name with the greatest love and reverence. This marriage gave him rank among the Makkan notables, while his conduct earned for him the surname al Amīn, the "Trustworthy."

The Makkans claimed descent from Abraham (Ibrahim) through Ishmael (Isma'il), and tradition stated that their temple (the Ka'bah) had been built by Ibrahim for the worship of the One God. It was still called the House of Allah, even though by the Prophet's time it housed the chief objects of the local pagan cult: several idols known as the "daughters of Allah" and regarded as intercessors. The few who were disgusted with the prevailing idolatry, which had prevailed for centuries, longed for the religion of Ibrahim and tried to discover its original teachings. Such seekers of the truth were known as Ḥunafā' (sing. Ḥanīf), a word that had originally meant "those who turn away" (from the existing idol-worship) but later on came to have the sense of "upright" or "by nature upright," because such persons held the way of truth to be right conduct. The Ḥunafā' did not form a community: they were the agnostics of their day, each seeking truth by the light of his own inner consciousness.

Muhammad became one of these people. It was his practice to retire for one month (Ramaḍān, the "month of heat") every year to a cave in the desert for meditation. His place of retreat was Ḥirā', a desert hill located close to Makkah. It was there one night toward the end of his retreat that the first revelation came to him when he was forty years old. He was asleep or in a trance when he heard a voice say: "Read!" He replied: "I cannot read." The voice again said: "Read!" and he again replied: "I cannot read." A third time, the voice commanded: "Read!" He said: "What can I read?" The voice said:

﴿اقْرَأْ بِاسْمِ رَبِّكَ الَّذِي خَلَقَ(١)خَلَقَ الإِنسَانَ مِنْ عَلَقٍ(٢)اقْرَأْ وَرَبُّكَ الأَكْرَمُ(٣)الَّذِي عَلَّمَ بِالْقَلَمِ(٤)عَلَّمَ الإِنسَانَ مَا لَمْ يَعْلَمْ﴾ (العلق: ١-٥).

Read: In the name of your Lord who creates, creates man from an *'alaq* (a clinging organism). Read: And your Lord is the Most Bounteous Who teaches by the pen, teaches man that which he knew not. (96:1–5)

When he awoke, the words remained "as if inscribed upon his heart." He went out of the cave and heard the same awe-inspiring voice say: "O Muhammad! You are Allah's Messenger, and I am Gabriel (Jibril)." Then he raised his eyes and saw the angel, in the likeness of a man, standing in the sky above the horizon. Again the awesome voice said: "O Muhammad! You are Allah's Messenger, and I am Gabriel." Muhammad (God's grace and peace be with him) stood quite still, turning his face away from the brightness of the vision. But wherever he turned his face, the angel was always standing there, confronting him. He remained thus a long while, until the angel vanished, and then returned in great distress to his wife Khadījah. She did her best to reassure him, saying that his conduct had been such that Allah would not let a harmful spirit come to him and that she hoped that he would become the prophet of his people. She took him to her cousin Waraqah ibn Nawfal, a very old man "who knew the Scriptures of Jews and Christians." This man declared his belief that the heavenly messenger who had come to Moses (Mūsā) had now come to Muhammad and that he had been chosen to serve as the prophet of his people.

To understand why the Prophet felt extreme distress after this, it must be remembered that the Ḥunafā' sought true religion in the natural world and distrusted any communication with those spirits about which men "avid of the Unseen" ﴿وَمَا هُوَ عَلَى الْغَيْبِ بِضَنِينٍ﴾ (81:24), sorcerers, soothsayers,

11

and even poets boasted in those days. Moreover, he was a man of humble and devout intelligence, a lover of quiet and solitude. The very thought of being chosen to face mankind alone with such a message at first appalled him. His recognition of the divine nature of the call caused a change in his whole mental outlook that was enough to disturb his sensitive and honest mind and caused him to forsake his quiet and honored way of life. The early biographers tell how Khadījah "tried the spirit" that came to him and proved it to be good, and how, when the revelations continued and his conviction in them grew, he at length accepted the tremendous task and was filled with an enthusiasm of obedience that justifies his proudest title: "The Slave of Allah."

The words that were revealed to him are held sacred by all Muslims and are never confounded with those uttered when no physical change was apparent in him. The former make up the Qur'an, while the latter form the Hadith or the Sunnah of the Prophet. Since the angel on Mt. Ḥirā' commanded him to "Read!" and insisted on his "reading", even though the Prophet was unlettered, the sacred book is known as al Qur'an, "The Reading," or "The Scripture" the Reading of the man who did not know how to read.

During the first three years of his mission, the Prophet preached only to his family and intimate friends. The people of Makkah as a whole regarded him as having become a little mad. His first convert was Khadījah, the second was his first cousin 'Alī (whom he had adopted), and the third was his servant Zayd (a former slave). His old friend Abū Bakr was among the early converts, along with some of his slaves and dependents.

At the end of the third year, the Prophet received the command to "arise and warn" ﴾فَقُمْ فَأَنذِرْ﴿ (74:2). He now began to preach in public, pointing out the wretched folly of idolatry in face of the tremendous laws of day and night, of life and death, of growth and decay, all of which manifest the power of Allah and attest to His sovereignty. When he began to speak against their gods, the Quraysh became actively hostile and began to persecute his poorer disciples and to mock and insult him. The one consideration that prevented them from killing him was their fear of the Prophet's clan's right to blood-vengence in the event of his murder. Strong in his inspiration, the Prophet continued to warn, plead, and threaten while the Quraysh did what they could to ridicule his teaching and spread dejection among his followers. The converts of the first four years were mostly humble folk who could not defend themselves. So cruel was the persecution they endured that the Prophet advised all who could possibly do so to emigrate to Abyssinia, a Christian country.[1]

---

1. In the fifth year of the Prophet's mission (the ninth year before the Prophet's flight to al Madinah), the Prophet allowed a number of the poorer converts to emigrate to Abyssinia, a Christian country, where they would not be persecuted for worshipping the One God. This is known as the first Hijrah. The rulers of Makkah sent ambassadors to ask the Negus (the local ruler) for their extradition. They were accused of having left the religion of their own people without entering the Christian religion and of having done wrong in their own country.

The Negus sent for the refugee's spokesmen, against the wish of the envoys, and in the presence of the bishops of his realm questioned them about their religion. Ja'far ibn Abī Ṭālib, the Prophet's cousin, answered:

We were folk immersed in ignorance, worshipping idols, eating carrion, given to lewdness, severing the ties of kinship, being bad neighbours, and the strong among us preyed upon the weak.

13

Despite the persecution and emigration, the number of Muslims grew. The Quraysh were seriously alarmed. The idol worship at the Ka'bah, the holy place to which all inhabitants of Arabia made pilgrimage and of which they were the guardian, was among their most important vested interests. During the pilgrimage season, they posted men on all the roads to warn the tribes against the madman preaching in their midst. They tried to persuade the Prophet to

---

Thus were we till Allah sent to us a messenger of our own, whose lineage, honesty, trustworthiness, and chastity we knew. He called us to Allah, that we should acknowledge His unity, worship Him, and eschew all the stones and idols that we and our fathers used to worship beside Him. He ordered us to be truthful, to restore the pledge, to observe the ties of kinship, to be good neighbours, to abstain from what is forbidden and from blood. He forbade us from lewdness and false speech, to prey upon the wealth of orphans, to accuse good women, and commanded us to worship Allah only, ascribing nothing unto Him as partner. He enjoined upon us prayer and legal alms and fasting. (And he enumerated for him the teachings of Islam.) So we trusted him, believed in him, and followed that which he had brought from Allah. We worshipped Allah only and ascribed no partner to Him. We refrained from that which was forbidden to us and indulged in that which was made lawful for us. Our people became hostile to us and tormented us. They sought to turn us from our religion that they might bring us back to the worship of idols from the worship of Allah Most High, and that we might indulge in those iniquities that before we had deemed lawful.

And when they persecuted and oppressed us, hemmed us in, and kept us from the practice of our religion, we came to your land. We chose you above all others, sought your protection, and hoped that we should not be troubled in your land, O King!

Then the Negus asked: "Do you have with you anything of that which he brought from his God?" Ja'far answered: "Yes." Then the Negus said: "Relate it to me." Ja'far recited the beginning verses of Surat Maryam. (Translated from the account given by Ibn Ishāq.)

14

compromise by offering to accept his religion if he would modify it to make room for their gods as intercessors with Allah. When this failed, they said that he could be their king if he would give up attacking idolatry. When their efforts at negotiation failed, they went to his uncle Abū Ṭālib and said that they would give him the best of their young men in place of Muhammad and, moreover, give him all that he desired, if only he would let them kill Muhammad. Abū Ṭālib refused.

The exasperation of the idolaters was increased by the conversion of 'Umar,[2] one of their stalwarts. They grew

---

2. In the early days of Islam, 'Umar ibn al Khaṭṭāb, who later became the second political successor of the Prophet, was one of Islam's bitterest opponents. One day, he went out with his sword intending to kill the Prophet, whom he referred to as "this Sabaean who has split the unity of Quraysh, calls their ideals foolish and their religion shameful, and blasphemes their gods." On the way, he met a friend who dissuaded him by reminding him that if he carried out his plan, he would have to reckon with the vengeance of a powerful clan—"Do you think that the Banū 'Abd Manāf would let you walk on the earth if you slew Muhammad?"—for tribal pride survived religious difference. He continued: "Is it not better for you to return to the folk of your own house and keep them straight?" 'Umar asked: "Which of the folk of my house?" "Your brother-in-law and cousin, Sa'īd ibn Zayd, and your sister, Fāṭimah bint al Khaṭṭāb. By Allah, they have become Muslims and followers of Muhammad in his religion. Look after them."

'Umar, enraged against his sister and brother-in-law, returned home and found with them Khabbāb ibn al 'Aratt. This man had a leaf on which was written (verses) from Surah Ṭā Hā and had been reading it aloud to them. When they heard 'Umar coming, Khabbāb hid in a closet and Fāṭimah hid the leaf under her thigh. But 'Umar had heard Khabbāb reading as he drew near the house. When he entered, he said: "What was that mumbling that I heard?" They said: "You heard nothing." 'Umar said: "By Allah! I have already been informed that you have become followers of Muhammad in his religion." Then he attacked his brother-in-law.

more and more embittered, till things came to such a pass that they decided to ostracize the Prophet's whole clan, regardless of whether or not they believed in his message. Their chief men drew up a document to the effect that none of them or their dependents would have any dealings, business or otherwise, with the Prophet's clan. They all signed this document and deposited it in the Ka'bah. For the next three years, the Prophet and his people were enclosed in their stronghold, which was located in one of the gorges leading to Makkah. Only at the time of pilgrimage could he go out and preach or did any of his kinsfolk dare go into the city.

Finally, some of the more sensitive members of the Quraysh grew weary of this boycott against their old friends

---

Fāṭimah sprang to keep him off her husband, and he struck and wounded her. When he had done that, his sister and his brother-in-law said to him: "Yes, we are Muslims and we believe in Allah and His messenger, so do what you will!" But when 'Umar saw the blood upon his sister, he was sorry for what he had done and said to his sister: "Give me that leaf from which I heard you reading just now, that I may see what Muhammad has brought." 'Umar was a scribe. When he said that, his sister said: "We fear to trust you with it." He said: "Fear not!" and swore by his gods that he would return it to her after he had read it. When he said that, she hoped for his conversion to Islam.

After he had read it, he said: "How excellent are these words!" and praised it highly. When he heard that, Khabbāb came out to him and said: "O 'Umar, I hope that Allah has brought you in answer to the prayer of the Prophet, for only yesterday I heard him saying: O Allah! Strengthen Islam with Abū al Ḥakam ibn Hishām or 'Umar ibn al Khaṭṭāb; and Allah is Allah, O 'Umar!" At that he said: "O Khabbāb, direct me to Muhammad that I may go to him and become a Muslim."

The conversion of 'Umar took place in the fifth year of the Prophet's mission (the ninth year before the Hijrah), soon after the departure of the emigrants to Abyssinia.

and neighbors. They managed to have the document brought out of the Ka'bah for reconsideration. It was then discovered that all of the writing had been destroyed by white ants, except for the words *Bismika Allāhuma* ("In Your name, O God"). When the elders saw this miracle, they lifted the ban and allowed the Prophet to resume his former way of life in the city. However, as the opposition to his preaching had grown rigid, he had little success among the Makkans. In addition, his attempt to preach in the city of al Tā'if also ended in failure. Judged by worldly standards, his mission was a failure.

But then he met a small group of men who listened to him and believed. They came from Yathrib, a city more than two hundred miles away, which has since become famous as *madīnat al Nabī* (the city of the Prophet) or *al Madinah*, "the City" par excellence. Among Yathrib's inhabitants were Jewish tribes whose learned rabbis had often spoken to the Arab pagans of a soon-to-come prophet who, along with the Jews, would destroy them as the tribes of 'Ād and Thamūd had been destroyed for their idolatry. After this group of men listened to Muhammad, they recognized him as the prophet described by the Jewish rabbis. On their return to Yathrib, they told others what they had seen and heard. As a result, when the next season of pilgrimage arrived, a deputation came from Yathrib in order to meet the Prophet. Its members swore allegiance to him in the first pact of al 'Aqabah. (This oath was afterwards exacted from female converts. It did not mention fighting, which was a later requirement for men.) They returned to Yathrib with a Muslim teacher in their company (Muṣ'ab ibn 'Umayr), and soon "there was not a house in Yathrib wherein the Messenger of Allah was not mentioned."

17

In the following year at the time of pilgrimage, seventy-three Muslims from Yathrib came to Makkah to swear allegiance to the Prophet and invite him to their city. At al 'Aqabah, they swore to defend him as they would their own wives and children. It was then that the Hijrah, or the Flight to Yathrib, was decided.

Soon those Muslims who could began to sell their property and leave Makkah unobtrusively. The Quraysh eventually learned what was going on and, although they hated having Muhammad in their midst, they were even more afraid of what he might do if he was beyond their reach. They decided that it would be better to kill him as soon as possible. When his chief protector, Abū Ṭālib, was removed by death, they saw their chance, even though they would still have to reckon with the vengeance of his clan. To avoid this, they cast lots and chose one member from every clan to participate in the attack on the Prophet. These men then pledged themselves to strike the Prophet at exactly the same time, so that his blood would be on the entire Quraysh tribes. It was at this time (aserts Ibn Khaldūn, and it is the only satisfactory explanation of what happened afterwards) that the Prophet received the first revelation ordering him to make war upon his persecutors "until persecution is no more and religion is for Allah only" ﴿حَتَّى لا تَكُونَ فِتْنَةٌ وَيَكُونَ الدِّينُ كُلُّهُ لِلَّهِ﴾ (8:39).

The last of the able Muslims in Makkah were Abū Bakr, 'Alī, and the Prophet. Abū Bakr, who was a wealthy man, had bought two riding camels and retained a guide in readiness for the Prophet's departure, which would take place when Allah ordered it.

18

On the appointed night, the murderers gathered in front of the Prophet's house. The Prophet gave his cloak to 'Alī and asked him to lie down on the bed so that if anyone looked in, they would think that it was the Prophet lying there. The murderers had decided to attack the Prophet whenever he came out of his house. Knowing that they would not injure 'Alī, the Prophet left the house unseen by his opponents. It is said that blindness fell upon the would-be murderers: he put dust on their heads as he passed by without them being aware of his departure. After picking up Abū Bakr at the latter's house, the two men went to a cave in the nearby mountains and stayed there until the immediate danger was past. Abū Bakr's son, daughter, and his herdsman brought them food and news after nightfall. The Makkans sent out search parties, one of which came quite near to their hiding place. Seeing that Abū Bakr was afraid, the Prophet told him: "Fear not! Allah is with us" ﴾ لَا تَحْزَنْ إِنَّ اللَّهَ مَعَنَا ﴿ (9:40). When the coast was clear, Abū Bakr told the guide to bring the riding camels to the cave one night so that they could begin the long ride to Yathrib.

After travelling for many days by unfrequented paths, the fugitives reached a suburb of Yathrib. The people of the city had been going there every morning for weeks in anticipation of the Prophet's arrival. They would give up their watch only when it became so hot that they had to seek shelter. It was at just such a time that the two travellers arrived. The man who spread the news was a Jew, who called out to the Muslims in derisive tones that the men for whom they were waiting had arrived at last. Such was the Hijrah, the Flight from Makkah to Yathrib, which marks the beginning of the Muslim era. The thirteen years of humiliation, perse-

19

cution, apparent failure, unfufilled prophecies were now over. The ten years of success, the fullest period that has ever crowned one man's endeavor, would now begin.

The Hijrah marks a clear division in the story of the Prophet's mission, which is evident in the Qur'an. Up until this time, he had only been a preacher. From now on, he would be the ruler of a state, admittedly at first a very small one, but one that would grow during the next ten years into the empire of Arabia. The kind of guidance that he and his people needed after the Hijrah was different from that which they had received in Makkah. Therefore, the surahs revealed during this period differ from those revealed earlier. Whereas the Makkan surahs give guidance to the individual soul and to the Prophet in his capacity as a warner, the Madinan surahs give guidance to a growing social and political community and to the Prophet as example, lawgiver, and reformer.

For classification purposes, the Makkan surahs are subdivided into four groups: very early, early, middle, and late. Though the historical data and traditions are insufficient for a strict chronological grouping, the very early surahs were, roughly speaking, revealed before the persecution began; the early surahs were revealed between the beginning of the persecution and 'Umar's conversion; the middle surahs were revealed between 'Umar's conversion and the destruction of the deed of ostracism; and the late surahs were revealed between the end of the ostracism and the Hijrah.

AT AL MADINAH

In the first year of his reign at Yathrib, the Prophet and the Jews negotiated a solemn treaty by which the latter were given full rights of citizenship and religious liberty in exchange for their support of the new state. However, their idea of a prophet was an individual who would give them dominion over others, not one who would make those who followed the same message (i.e., Arab Muslims) their brothers and equals. When they discovered that they could not use the Prophet for their own purposes, they tried to weaken his faith in his mission and to seduce his followers. They received secret support for these efforts from some professing Muslims who thought that the presence of the Prophet in their city would weaken or even end their influence and therefore resented his presence. In the Madinan surahs, such Jews and Hypocrites are mentioned with great frequency.

Until this time, the *qiblah* (the place toward which Muslims face when praying) had been Jerusalem. The Jews, believing that this implied a pro-Judaism bias on the part of the Prophet, began to say that he needed to be instructed by them. To clear up this misunderstanding, it was revealed to the Prophet that the Muslims should turn their faces towards Makkah and the Ka'bah when praying. The Qur'an says:

21

﴿قَدْ نَرَى تَقَلُّبَ وَجْهِكَ فِي السَّمَاءِ فَلَنُوَلِّيَنَّكَ قِبْلَةً تَرْضَاهَا فَوَلِّ وَجْهَكَ شَطْرَ الْمَسْجِدِ الْحَرَامِ وَحَيْثُ مَا كُنْتُمْ فَوَلُّوا وُجُوهَكُمْ شَطْرَهُ وَإِنَّ الَّذِينَ أُوتُوا الْكِتَابَ لَيَعْلَمُونَ أَنَّهُ الْحَقُّ مِنْ رَبِّهِمْ وَمَا اللَّهُ بِغَافِلٍ عَمَّا يَعْمَلُونَ(١٤٤)وَلَئِنْ أَتَيْتَ الَّذِينَ أُوتُوا الكِتَابَ بِكُلِّ آيَةٍ مَا تَبِعُوا قِبْلَتَكَ وَمَا أَنْتَ بِتَابِعٍ قِبْلَتَهُمْ وَمَا بَعْضُهُمْ بِتَابِعٍ قِبْلَةَ بَعْضٍ وَلَئِنِ اتَّبَعْتَ أَهْوَاءَهُمْ مِنْ بَعْدِ مَا جَاءَكَ مِنَ الْعِلْمِ إِنَّكَ إِذًا لَمِنَ الظَّالِمِينَ(١٤٥)الَّذِينَ آتَيْنَاهُمُ الْكِتَابَ يَعْرِفُونَهُ كَمَا يَعْرِفُونَ أَبْنَاءَهُمْ وَإِنَّ فَرِيقًا مِنْهُمْ لَيَكْتُمُونَ الْحَقَّ وَهُمْ يَعْلَمُونَ(١٤٦)الْحَقُّ مِنْ رَبِّكَ فَلَا تَكُونَنَّ مِنَ الْمُمْتَرِينَ(١٤٧)وَلِكُلٍّ وِجْهَةٌ هُوَ مُوَلِّيهَا فَاسْتَبِقُوا الْخَيْرَاتِ أَيْنَ مَا تَكُونُوا يَأْتِ بِكُمُ اللَّهُ جَمِيعًا إِنَّ اللَّهَ عَلَى كُلِّ شَيْءٍ قَدِيرٌ(١٤٨)وَمِنْ حَيْثُ خَرَجْتَ فَوَلِّ وَجْهَكَ شَطْرَ الْمَسْجِدِ الْحَرَامِ وَإِنَّهُ لَلْحَقُّ مِنْ رَبِّكَ وَمَا اللَّهُ بِغَافِلٍ عَمَّا تَعْمَلُونَ(١٤٩)وَمِنْ حَيْثُ خَرَجْتَ فَوَلِّ وَجْهَكَ شَطْرَ الْمَسْجِدِ الْحَرَامِ وَحَيْثُ مَا كُنْتُمْ فَوَلُّوا وُجُوهَكُمْ شَطْرَهُ لِئَلَّا يَكُونَ لِلنَّاسِ عَلَيْكُمْ حُجَّةٌ إِلَّا الَّذِينَ ظَلَمُوا مِنْهُمْ فَلَا تَخْشَوْهُمْ وَاخْشَوْنِي وَلِأُتِمَّ نِعْمَتِي عَلَيْكُمْ وَلَعَلَّكُمْ تَهْتَدُونَ﴾ (البقرة: ١٤٤-١٥٠).

We have seen the turning of your face to heaven (for guidance, O Muhammad). And now surely We shall make you turn (in prayer) toward a *qiblah* which is dear to you. So turn your face toward the Sacred Mosque (the Ka'bah in Makkah), and you (O Muslims), wheresoever you may be, turn your faces (when you pray) toward it. Lo! those who have received the Scripture know that (this Revelation) is the Truth from their Lord. And Allah is not unaware of what they do.

And even if you bring unto those who have received the Scripture all kinds of portents, they would not follow your *qiblah,* nor can you be a follower of their *qiblah;*

22

nor are some of them followers of the *qiblah* of others. And if you should follow their desires after the knowledge which has come unto you, then surely were you of the evildoers.

Those unto whom We gave the Scripture recognize (this revelation) as they recognize their children. But lo! a party of them knowingly conceal the truth.

It is the Truth from your Lord (O Muhammad), so be not you of those who waver.

And each one has a goal toward which he turns; so vie with one another in good works. Wheresoever you may be, Allah will bring you all together. Lo! Allah is Able to do all things.

And whencesoever you come forth (for prayer, O Muhammad) turn your face toward the Sacred Mosque. Lo! it is the Truth from your Lord. Allah is not unaware of what you do.

Whencesoever you come forth turn your face toward the Sacred Mosque; and wheresoever you may be (O Muslims) turn your faces toward it (when you pray) so that men may have no argument against you, save such of them as do injustice—Fear them not, but fear Me—so that I may complete My grace upon you, and that you may be guided. (2:144–150)

The whole first part of the second surah in the Qur'an deals with this Jewish controversy.

Now that he was a ruler, the Prophet's first concern was to establish public worship and to lay down his state's constitution. He did not forget, however, that the Quraysh had sworn to oppose his religion or that he had been ordered by Allah to fight against his persecutors until they were completely defeated. One year after his arrival in Yathrib, he sent out small expeditions, led by himself or someone else, in order to see what was going on and to persuade other local tribes not to side with the Quraysh.

These are generally represented as warlike but, considering their weakness and the fact that there was no actual fighting (although they were prepared to fight), they can hardly have been that. It is noteworthy that these expeditions were composed only of Muslims who had originally come from Makkah. The natives of Yathrib did not participate for the reason that (if we accept Ibn Khaldūn's theory) the command to fight had been revealed to the Prophet at Makkah after the men from Yathrib had sworn their oath of allegiance at al 'Aqabah. They had undertaken to protect the Prophet from attack, not to fight with him in actual campaigns. Blood was shed and booty taken—against the Prophet's express orders—in only one of those early expeditions. One purpose of those expeditions may have been to prepare the Makkan Muslims for actual warfare. For thirteen years they had been strict pacifists and it is clear from several Qur'anic passages that many, including perhaps even the Prophet, hated the idea of fighting even in self-defence and had to accept it gradually. Allah says in the Qur'an:

﴿كُتِبَ عَلَيْكُمُ الْقِتَالُ وَهُوَ كُرْهٌ لَكُمْ وَعَسَى أَنْ تَكْرَهُوا شَيْئًا وَهُوَ خَيْرٌ لَكُمْ وَعَسَى أَنْ تُحِبُّوا شَيْئًا وَهُوَ شَرٌّ لَكُمْ وَاللَّهُ يَعْلَمُ وَأَنْتُمْ لاَ تَعْلَمُونَ﴾

(البقرة: ٢١٦).

Warfare is ordained for you, though it is hateful unto you; but it may happen that you hate a thing which is good for you, and it may happen that you love a thing

24

which is bad for you. Allah knows, you know not. (2:216)

In the second year of the Hijrah, a caravan belonging to Makkan merchants was returning from Syria by the usual route, which happened to be located not far from Yathrib. Its leader, Abū Sufyān, learned of the Prophet's plan to capture the caravan as he approached the territory of Yathrib. At once he sent a camel-rider to Makkah. Upon his arrival, the exhausted rider shouted frantically from the valley to the Quraysh to ride as fast as they could to protect their wealth and honor. A force of one thousand warriors was soon on its way to Yathrib—apparently less concerned with saving the caravan than with punishing the raiders, since the Prophet might have taken the caravan before their departure.

Did the Prophet ever intend to raid the caravan? According to Ibn Hishām's account of the Tābūk expedition, on that one occasion the Prophet did not hide his real objective. The caravan was the pretext for the campaign of Badr, and the real objective was the Makkan army. He had received the command to fight his persecutors, had been promised victory, and was ready to fight against all odds (as was the case with the battle of Badr). The Muslims, until then not very eager for war and also ill-equipped, would have despaired if they had known at the outset that they would face a well-armed force three times their number.

The Quraysh army advanced more than half-way to Yathrib before the Prophet set out. The two armies, in addition to the caravan, were all heading for the water located at Badr. Abū Sufyān, the caravan leader, heard from one of his scouts that the Muslims were near the water and so turned back to the coastal plain. The Muslims met the Quraysh by the water. Before the battle, the Prophet was prepared to increase the odds against him. He told the *Anṣār* (his supporters among the natives of Yathrib) that they could return to their homes unreproached, since their oath did not include participating in actual warfare. The *Anṣār,* however, were hurt by the very thought that they would even consider leaving the Prophet when he was in danger.

Despite the clear difference in numbers in favor of the Quraysh, Muslims emerged victorious.[3] This victory gave

---

3.   A Makkan caravan was returning from Syria. Its leader, Abū Sufyān, feared an attack from al Madinah and therefore sent a rider to Makkah with a frantic appeal for help. This must have come too late if, considering the distances involved and the claim even by some Muslim writers, that the Prophet had always intended to attack the caravan. Ibn Isḥāq (Ibn Hishām), when dealing with the Tabūk expedition, says that the Prophet announced the destination, which was a departure from his usual practice of concealing the real objective.

Was not the real objective hidden in this first campaign? It is a fact that he advanced only when the army sent to protect the caravan, or rather—probably—to punish the Muslims for having plundered it, was approaching al Madinah. His little army of three hundred and thirteen ill-armed and roughly equipped men traversed the desert for three days, halting only when they were near the water of Badr. There, they learned that the Quraysh army was approaching on the other side of the valley. Rain began to fall heavily on the Quraysh, and the resulting muddy ground made it impossible for them to advance any further. The Muslims took advantage of this situation and secured the water. At the same time, Abū Sufyān, whose caravan was also heading for the water of Badr, was warned of the Muslim advance by a scout and thus turned back to the coastal plain. Before the battle against what must have seemed to be overwhelming odds, the Prophet gave the *Anṣār* (the men of al Madinah whose oath of allegiance had not included participating in actual warfare) the chance of returning if they wished. The mere suggestion that they could possibly forsake him hurt them. On the other hand, several men of

26

the Prophet new prestige among the Arab tribes, but it also resulted in a blood feud, in addition to the religious conflict, between the Quraysh and the Prophet. The Qur'anic passages that refer to the battle of Badr warn of much greater struggles to come.

In fact, the very next year saw an army of three thousand Makkan warriors on their way to Yathrib to destroy it.

Quraysh, including the whole Zuhrī clan, returned to Makkah when they heard that the caravan was safe. They held no grudge against the Prophet and his followers, whom they regarded as men who had been wronged.

Still, the Quraysh army outnumbered the Muslims by more than two to one and was much better mounted and equipped. Therefore its leaders expected an easy victory. When the Prophet saw them streaming down the sandhills, he cried: "O Allah! Here are the Quraysh with all their chivalry and pomp, who oppose You and deny Your messenger. O Allah! Your help which You have promised me! O Allah! Make them bow this day!"

Although the Muslims were successful in the single combat with which Arab battles opened, the real battle at first went hard against them. The Prophet stood and prayed under a shelter that had been constructed to screen him from the sun: "O Allah! If this little company is destroyed, there will be none left in the land to worship You." Then he fell into a trance and, when he spoke again, informed Abu Bakr, who was with him, that the promised help had come. Thereupon he went out to encourage his people. Taking up a handful of gravel, he ran towards the Quraysh and flung it at them, saying: "The faces are confounded!" The tide of battle now turned in favor of the Muslims. The Quraysh's leader and several of its greatest men were killed, many were taken prisoner, and their baggage and camels were captured by the Muslims.

It was indeed a day to be remembered in the early history of Islam, and there was great rejoicing in al Madinah. However, the Muslims were warned that this was only the beginning of their struggle against heavy odds. In fact, in the following year at Mt. Uḥud, the enemy army three thousand strong took the field against them. In the year 5 A.H., a ten thousand man strong allied army of the pagan clans besieged al Madinah in the "War of the Trench" (see Surah 33, "The Clans").

27

The Prophet's first idea was to defend the city. This plan received the strong support of 'Abd Allāh ibn 'Ubayy, leader of "the Hypocrites" (or lukewarm Muslims). However, the veterans of Badr believed that God would help them against any odds and thought they would shame themselves if they remained behind walls. The Prophet, approving of their faith and zeal, agreed and set out with one thousand men toward the enemy encampment at Mt. Uḥud. 'Abd Allāh ibn 'Ubayy opposed this change in plan, for he thought it unlikely that the Pro-phet would really fight in such disadvantageous circumstances and did not want to take part in a demonstration designed to appease fanatical extremists. He therefore withdrew with his men and decreased the size of the Muslim army by one-third.

Despite the heavy odds, the battle at Mt. Uḥud would have been an even greater Muslim victory than that at Badr if the band of fifty Muslim archers, whom the Prophet set to guard a pass against the enemy cavalry, had not deserted their posts upon seeing their comrades victorious, fearing that they might miss out on the resulting spoils. The Quraysh cavalry rode through the gap, fell on the exultant Muslims, and wounded the Prophet. The cry arose that the Prophet had been killed. However, someone recognized him and shouted that he was still living, which caused the demoralized Muslims to rally. They gathered around the Prophet and began to retreat, leaving many fallen warriors on the hillside.[4]

---

4. In 3 A.H. the Makkans attacked al Madinah with an army of 3,000 men in order to avenge their defeat at Badr the previous year and to wipe out the Muslims. The Prophet, who at first had planned to defend al Madinah, decided, at the insistence of his Companions, to meet the enemy

On the following day, the Prophet again sallied forth with what remained of his army so that the Quraysh would hear that he was in the field and perhaps be deterred from attacking the city. The stratagem succeeded, thanks to a friendly bedouin who, after meeting and talking with the Muslims, encountered the Quraysh. Upon being questioned by Abū Sufyān, he said that Muhammad was in the field, stronger than ever, and thirsting for revenge. Based on this information, Abū Sufyān decided to return to Makkah.

This reverse lowered the Muslims' prestige with the Arab tribes and also with the Jews of Yathrib. Tribes that had inclined towards the Muslims now inclined towards the Quraysh. The Prophet's followers were attacked and mur-

---

at Mt. Uḥud and thus stationed his men carefully. He led an army of 1,000 men, a third of whom under 'Abd Allāh ibn 'Ubayy (the "hypocrite" leader) deserted him before the battle and said afterwards that they had thought that there would be no fighting that day. The battle began well for the Muslims, but was changed to something near defeat by the disobedience of a band of fifty archers placed to guard a certain point. Seeing the Muslims winning, they feared that they might lose their share of the spoils and so ran to join the others. Their action left an opening for the Makkan cavalry, and the idolaters managed to rally and inflict considerable loss upon the Muslims. The Prophet himself was wounded. A cry arose that the Prophet had been killed, and the Muslims were in despair until someone recognized the Prophet and cried out that he was still alive. The Muslims then rallied to his side and retired in some sort of order. The Quraysh army also retired after the battle.

The wives of the Qurayshī leaders, who had been brought with the army to encourage the men by their presence and their chanting, mutilated the Muslim corpses and made necklaces and bracelets of severed ears and noses. Hind, the wife of Abu Sufyān, extracted the liver of the Prophet's uncle, Hamzah, and tried to eat it. When the Prophet saw what was happening, he was moved to vow reprisal. But he was relieved of his vow by a revelation that forbade Muslims to mutilate the corpses of the enemy.

29

dered when they went abroad in little companies. Khubayb, an envoy of the Prophet, was captured by a desert tribe and sold to the Quraysh, who then tortured him to death before the people of Makkah. The Jews, despite their treaty with the Prophet, became almost open in their hostility and told the Quraysh that their pagan religion was superior to Islam. Allah says in the Qur'an:

﴿أَلَمْ تَرَ إِلَى الَّذِينَ أُوتُوا نَصِيبًا مِنْ الْكِتَابِ يُؤْمِنُونَ بِالْجِبْتِ وَالطَّاغُوتِ وَيَقُولُونَ لِلَّذِينَ كَفَرُوا هَؤُلَاءِ أَهْدَى مِنْ الَّذِينَ آمَنُوا سَبِيلاً﴾ (النساء: ٥١).

Have you not seen those unto whom a portion of the Scripture has been given, how they believe in idols and false deities, and how they say of those (idolaters) who disbelieve: "These are more rightly guided than those who believe?" (4:51)

The Prophet was obliged to take punitive action against some of them. The Banī al Naḍīr tribe was besieged in its strong forts, eventually subdued, and then forced to emigrate. The Hypocrites had sympathized with the Jews and encouraged them secretly.[5]

---

5. *Surat al Ḥashr*, "Exile," takes its name from verses 2-17, which refer to the exile of Banī al Naḍīr (for treason and attempted murder of the Prophet) and the confiscation of their property. The "hypocrites," as the lukewarm Muslims were called, had secretly sympathized with these Jews, whose opposition had grown strong since the Muslim reverse at Mt. Uḥud. The hypocrites had also promised to side with them in the event of armed hostilities with the Muslims and to emigrate with them if they were forced to emigrate. But when the Muslims marched against Banī al Naḍīr, and the latter took refuge in their strong towers, the hypocrites did nothing. When they were finally defeated and exiled, the hypocrites did not go with them.

In the fifth year of the Hijrah, the idolaters made a great effort to destroy Islam in an event called the War of the Clans or War of the Trench. The Quraysh gathered all of its clans and allied its army with that of the Ghaṭafān, a great desert tribe. This alliance, ten thousand warriors strong, then marched on Yathrib, by now known as al Madinah. The Prophet ordered (supposedly upon the advice of Salmān the Persian) and participated in the digging of a deep trench in front of the city. The enemy army did not know what to do when faced with such a novelty; they had never seen such a defense before. As their cavalry, which formed their strength, did not know how, or was unable, to breach it, they camped in sight of it and daily showered their arrows on its defenders.

While the Muslims awaited the assault, news came that Banī Qurayẓah, a Jewish tribe of Yathrib that had till then been loyal, had gone over to the enemy. The case seemed desperate. However, the delay caused by the trench had dampened the enemy's enthusiasm, and an individual who was secretely a Muslim was able to sow distrust between the Quraysh and their Jewish allies. This caused both sides to hesitate. During their hesitation, a bitter wind from the sea reached them. It engulfed them for three days and nights and was so strong that no tent could be kept standing, no fire lit, or no water boiled. Seing that the tribesmen were in utter misery, one night the leader of the Quraysh army decided that the torment could be borne no longer and gave the order to retire. When the Ghatafān awoke the next morning and saw that the Quraysh had departed, they gathered their supplies and retreated.[6]

---

6. When certain members of the Banī al Naḍīr whom the Prophet had expelled from Yathrib on grounds of treason, they went to the

31

Upon his return from the trench, the Prophet ordered war against the treacherous Banī Qurayẓah who, conscious of their guilt, had already taken to their towers of refuge. After a siege of nearly a month, they surrendered unconditionally and begged to be judged by a member of the Arab tribe to which they were affiliated. The Prophet granted their request and carried out the sentence of the judge: the execution of the men and the enslavement of the women and children.

---

leaders of Quraysh in Makkah and then to the chiefs of the great desert tribe of Ghaṭafān and urged them to extirpate the Muslims. They promised help from the Jewish population of Yathrib. As a result of their efforts, all of the Quraysh and the Ghaṭafān clans marched towards Yathrib to destroy it.

When news of their design reached the Prophet, he ordered a trench to be dug before the city and then himself led the project. The trench was finished when the clans arrived—10,000 strong. The Prophet took the field with his army of 3000, keeping the trench between the two armies. For nearly a month, the Muslims were exposed to showers of arrows and were in constant expectation of an attack by the far superior enemy forces. To make matters worse, news came that the Jewish tribe of Banī Qurayẓah in their rear had broken their alliance with the Muslims and joined the Quraysh. The women and children had been put in strongholds—towers like the peel-towers of northern England (every family of note had one for refuge in time of raids). These were practically unguarded, and some of the Muslims asked the Prophet's permission to leave the battlefront in order to guard them. These towers were not then in danger, because the Banī Qurayẓah were not likely to show their treachery until the clans' victory was certain.

The case of the Muslims seemed hopeless. However, a secret sympathiser (Nuʿaym ibn Masʿūd) in the enemy camp managed to sow distrust between the Banī Qurayẓah and the chiefs of the clans, making both feel uneasy. The obstacle of the trench was unexpected and seemed formidable. In addition, when a fierce and bitter wind from the Red Sea blew for three days and nights so furiously that they could not keep a shelter up, light a fire, or boil a pot of liquid, Abū Sufyān, the leader of Quraysh,

Early in the sixth year of the Hijrah, the Prophet led a campaign against the Banī al Muṣṭaliq tribe, as it had been preparing to attack the Muslims. During the return from this campaing, 'Ā'ishah, the Prophet's young wife, was left behind. A young soldier found her and brought her back to the Muslim camp. This incident gave rise to the scandal denounced in *Surah al Nūr* (24).

﴿إِنَّ الَّذِينَ جَاءُوا بِالإِفْكِ عُصْبَةٌ مِنْكُمْ لاَ تَحْسَبُوهُ شَرًّا لَكُمْ بَلْ هُوَ خَيْرٌ لَكُمْ لِكُلِّ امْرِئٍ مِنْهُمْ مَا اكْتَسَبَ مِنَ الأَثْمِ وَالَّذِي تَوَلَّى كِبْرَهُ مِنْهُمْ لَهُ عَذَابٌ عَظِيمٌ﴾ (النور: ١١).

Lo! they who spread the slander are a gang among you. Deem it not a bad thing for you; nay, it is good for you. Unto every man of them will be paid that which he has earned of the sin; and as for him among them who had

---

raised the siege in disgust. When the Ghaṭafān learned that the Quraysh had gone, they also departed for their homes.

On the very day when the Muslims returned from the trench, they besieged the traitorous Banī Qurayzah in their towers of refuge for twenty-five days. After they surrendered, some members of the 'Aws tribe, of which they were members, asked the Prophet to show them the same grace that he had shown to the tribe of Khazraj, in the case of Banī al Naḍir, by allowing them to intercede for their dependents.

The Prophet said: "Would you like one of your own to decide their fate?" They said: "Yes," and he appointed Sa'd ibn Mu'ādh, a great chief of the 'Aws who had been wounded and was being cared for in the mosque. This man was sent for and, after hearing the case, ordered their men to be put to death, their women and children to be made captive, and their property to be divided among the Muslims as the Prophet directed.

I have taken this account from the narrative of Ibn Khaldūn, which is concise, rather than from Ibn Hishām, which is exceedingly diffuse. The two accounts are, however, in absolute agreement. Verses 33:26–27 refer to the punishment of the Banī Qurayzah.

the greater share therein, his will be an awful doom. (24:11)

In addition, 'Abd Allāh ibn 'Ubayy, the "Hypocrite" chief, planned to exploit the situation. He is reported to have said: "When we return to the city the mightier will soon expel the weaker" ﴿لَئِنْ رَجَعْنَا إِلَى الْمَدِينَةِ لَيُخْرِجَنَّ الأَعَزُّ مِنْهَا الأَذَلَّ﴾ (63:8), upon witnessing a quarrel between the Muhājirīn (immigrants from Makkah) and the Anṣār (natives of Yathrib).

In the same year, the Prophet had a vision in which he saw himself entering the holy precincts of Makkah unopposed and made the intention to perform the pilgrimage.

﴿لَقَدْ صَدَقَ اللَّهُ رَسُولَهُ الرُّؤْيَا بِالْحَقِّ لَتَدْخُلُنَّ الْمَسْجِدَ الْحَرَامَ إِنْ شَاءَ اللَّهُ آمِنِينَ مُحَلِّقِينَ رُءُوسَكُمْ وَمُقَصِّرِينَ لَا تَخَافُونَ فَعَلِمَ مَا لَمْ تَعْلَمُوا فَجَعَلَ مِنْ دُونِ ذَلِكَ فَتْحًا قَرِيبًا﴾ (الفتح: ٢٧).

Allah has fulfilled the vision for His Messenger in very truth. You shall indeed enter the Sacred Mosque, if Allah will, secure, (having your hair) shaven and cut, not fearing. But He knows that which you know not, and has given you a near victory beforehand. (48:27)

Along with a number of Muslims from Yathrib (which we shall hereafter call al Madinah), he called upon those Arabs who were sympathetic to his cause, whose numbers had increased since the miraculous (as it was considered) discomfiture of the clans, to accompany him. Most of them did not respond. Allah says in the Qur'an:

﴿سَيَقُولُ لَكَ الْمُخَلَّفُونَ مِنَ الأَعْرَابِ شَغَلَتْنَا أَمْوَالُنَا وَأَهْلُونَا فَاسْتَغْفِرْ
لَنَا يَقُولُونَ بِأَلْسِنَتِهِمْ مَا لَيْسَ فِي قُلُوبِهِمْ قُلْ فَمَنْ يَمْلِكُ لَكُمْ مِنَ اللَّهِ
شَيْئًا إِنْ أَرَادَ بِكُمْ ضَرًّا أَوْ أَرَادَ بِكُمْ نَفْعًا بَلْ كَانَ اللَّهُ بِمَا تَعْمَلُونَ
خَبِيرًا﴾ (الفتح: ١١).

Those of the wandering Arabs who were left behind will
tell you: Our possessions and our households occupied
us, so ask forgiveness for us! They speak with their
tongues that which is not in their hearts. Say: Who can
avail you anything against Allah, if He intends you hurt
or intends you profit? Nay, but Allah is ever Aware of
what you do. (48:11)

This did not deter him, however, and he set out for Makkah
with fourteen hundred men attired as pilgrims and bearing
the customary offerings. As they approached the holy valley, they were met by a friend from the city who warned the
Prophet that the Quraysh had put on their leopardskins (a
badge of valor), had sworn to prevent him from entering the
sanctuary, and that their cavalry was on the road in front of
him. After hearing this, the Prophet ordered a detour
through mountain gorges. When his exhausted troops finally reached al Ḥudaybīyah, a site located within the valley of
Makkah, they set up camp and rested.

The Prophet now sought to open negotiations. He sent a
messenger to the enemy camp to inform the Quraysh that he
and his men wanted to enter Makkah only as pilgrims. This
man was maltreated, his camel was hamstrung, and he had
to return before he could deliver his message. The Quraysh
then sent a man to convey their message in a very threatening and arrogant tone. Another of their messengers was too

familiar and had to be reminded sternly of the respect due to the Prophet. When this second messenger returned to Makkah, he said: "I have seen Caesar and Chosroes in their pomp, but never have I seen a man so honored by his comrades as is Muhammad."

The Prophet decided to send another messenger whom the Quraysh would be forced to treat with respect. Eventually, he chose to send 'Uthmān ibn 'Affān, who had ties of kinship with the powerful 'Umayyad family. While the Muslims were awaiting his return, they received the news that he had been murdered. This turn of events caused the Prophet, who was sitting under a tree at al Ḥudaybīyah, to bind his followers to an oath that they would all stand or fall together. Allah says:

﴿ إِنَّ الَّذِينَ يُبَايِعُونَكَ إِنَّمَا يُبَايِعُونَ اللَّهَ يَدُ اللَّهِ فَوْقَ أَيْدِيهِمْ فَمَنْ نَكَثَ فَإِنَّمَا يَنْكُثُ عَلَى نَفْسِهِ وَمَنْ أَوْفَى بِمَا عَاهَدَ عَلَيْهُ اللَّهَ فَسَيُؤْتِيهِ أَجْرًا عَظِيمًا ﴾ (الفتح: ١٠)

Lo! those who swear allegiance unto you (Muhammad), swear allegiance only unto Allah. The Hand of Allah is above their hands. So whosoever breaks his oath, breaks it only to his soul's hurt; while whosoever keeps his covenant with Allah, on him will He bestow immense reward. (48:10)

After a while, however, it became known that 'Uthmān had not been murdered. A group of Makkan warriors that tried to harm the Muslims in their camp was captured before any harm was done, and the men were forgiven and released after they promised the Prophet that they would renounce their previous hostility. In the Qur'an Allah says:

36

﴿وَهُوَ الَّذِي كَفَّ أَيْدِيَهُمْ عَنكُمْ وَأَيْدِيَكُمْ عَنْهُم بِبَطْنِ مَكَّةَ مِنْ بَعْدِ أَنْ أَظْفَرَكُمْ عَلَيْهِمْ وَكَانَ اللَّهُ بِمَا تَعْمَلُونَ بَصِيرًا﴾ (الفتح: ٢٤).

And He it is Who has withheld men's hands from you, and has withheld your hands from them, in the valley of Makkah, after He had made you victors over them. Allah is Seer of what you do. (48:24)

This incident marked the beginning of serious negotiations, for the Quraysh now sent proper envoys. The resulting agreement, known as the truce of al Ḥudaybīyah, enshrined a cessation of hostilities for a period of ten years. The Prophet was to return to al Madinah without visiting the Ka'bah with the understanding that he and his comrades would be able to perform the pilgrimage the following year. At that time, the Quraysh would evacuate Makkah for three days so that his pilgrimage could be made properly. The Prophet promised to return all members of the Quraysh who sought to join the Muslims, even though the Quraysh did not have to assume a corresponding obligation. It was also accepted by both sides that any tribe or clan that wished to participate in the treaty as allies of the Prophet or of the Quraysh could do so.

There was dismay among the Muslims when they learned of the terms. They asked one another: "Where is the victory that we were promised?" In response, *Surat al Fath* (Victory) was revealed while the troops were returning to al Madinah.[7] What these men did not know was that this truce

---

7. *Al Fath* takes its name from the word *fath*, which means "victory." It occurs several times and refers not to the conquest of Makkah but

would prove to be the greatest victory achieved by the
Muslims up to that time, for armed hostilities, which had

---

to the truce of al Ḥudaybīyah. Although thought at the time a setback to
the Muslims, it proved in fact to be the greatest victory for Islam.

In the year 6 A.H., the Prophet set out with some 1,400 Muslims from
al Madinah and the surrounding countryside. They were dressed for pilgrimage, not war, and wanted to visit the Ka‘bah. When they drew close
to Makkah, they were warned that the Quraysh had gathered their allies
and that their cavalry, led by Khālid ibn al Walīd, was on the road before
them. Making a detour through gullies of the hills, the Muslims eluded the
cavalry and, coming into the valley of Makkah, they encamped at al
Ḥudaybīyah (below the city). The Prophet resolutely refused to fight and
persisted in attempts to talk with the Quraysh, who had sworn not to let
him reach the Ka‘bah. The Muslims were in a position of some danger.
Finally ‘Uthmān ibn ‘Affān was sent into the city, for it was thought that
he was the most likely to be well received on account of his relationships.
‘Uthmān was detained by the Makkans, and news that he had been murdered reached the Muslim camp.

It was then that the Prophet, sitting under a tree, took from his comrades the oath (referred to in 48:18) that they would hold together and
fight to the death. It then became known that the rumor of ‘Uthmān's
death was false. Finally, the Quraysh agreed to a truce whose terms were
favorable to themselves. The Prophet and his followers were to give up
the project of visiting the sanctuary for that year, but could make the pilgrimage the following year when the idolaters would evacuate Makkah
for three days. People who ran away from the Quraysh to the Muslim
camp would be returned, but people who ran away from the Muslims to
the Quraysh would not be returned. In addition, there was to be no hostility between the parties for ten years.

"And there was never a victory," says Ibn Khaldūn, "greater than this
victory, for as al Zuhrī says, when it was war the peoples did not meet,
but when the truce came and war laid down its burdens, the people felt
safe one with another and so they met and talked with each other. No man
spoke of Islam to another but the latter embraced it, so that in the inter-
vening two years (i.e., between al Ḥudaybīyah and the breaking of the
truce by the Quraysh), the number of people who became Muslim was
equal to or more than the number of those who had already become
Muslim."

been a barrier between them and the non-Muslims, had prevented both parties from meeting and talking with each other. Now that this barrier had been removed, the new religion spread more rapidly. In the two years that elapsed between the signing of the truce and the fall of Makkah, more people embraced Islam than had done so since the beginning of the Prophet's mission. The Prophet had travelled to al Huday-bīyah with 1400 men. Two years later, when the Makkans broke the truce, he marched against them with an army of ten thousand.

In the seventh year of the Hijrah, the Prophet led a campaign against the Jewish stronghold of Khaybar, which was located in northern Arabia and had become a focal point for his enemies. The forts of Khaybar were reduced one by one, and their Jewish inhabitants were turned into tenants of the Muslims until all Jews were expelled from Arabia during the caliphate of 'Umar. On the day when the last fort surrendered, Ja'far, son of Abū Ṭālib and the Prophet's cousin, arrived from Abyssinia with the Muslims whom the Prophet had advised to leave Makkah fifteen years earliers.

After the Muslims' victory at Khaybar, a Jewess prepared a meal of poisoned meat for the Prophet. He tasted, but did not swallow, a small piece of it and then told his comrades that it was poisoned. One Muslim, who had already swallowed some of it, died instantly. The Prophet, even though he had only tasted it, contracted the illness that eventually caused his death. When the guilty woman was brought before him, she said that she had done it to avenge the humiliation of her people. The Prophet forgave her.

During this same year, the Prophet's vision was fulfilled; he visited the holy place at Makkah unopposed. In accordance with the terms of the truce, the non-Muslims evacuated the city and watched the Muslim pilgrimage from the surrounding heights. At the end of the stipulated three days, the chiefs of the Quraysh sent word to the Prophet to remind him that they had fulfilled their part of the treaty and that it was now time for him to leave Makkah. He withdrew, and the idolaters reoccupied the city.

In the eighth year of the Hijrah, hearing that the Byzantine emperor was gathering a force in Syria to send against the Muslims, the Prophet dispatched three thousand men under the command of his freedman Zayd. The campaign was not successful, but the reckless valor of the Muslims—three thousand of them did not hesitate to take the battle field against one hundred thousand enemy troops—left an impression on the Syrians. When all of the three leaders appointed by the Prophet had been killed, the survivors obeyed Khālid ibn al Walīd, whose strategy and courage preserved the Muslim army and got it back to al Madinah.

Also in this year, the Quraysh broke the truce by attacking a tribe allied to the Prophet and massacring its members even in the sanctuary at Makkah. After this breach, the Quraysh sent Abū Sufyān to al Madinah to ask for the existing treaty to be renewed and prolonged before the Prophet learned what had happened to his allies. His mission ended in failure, however, for a survivor was able to reach the Prophet and inform him of the massacre.

The Prophet now summoned all of the Muslims who could bear arms and marched on Makkah. The Quraysh were overwhelmed and, after putting up a show of defense in front of the town, were routed without bloodshed. The

Prophet, upon entering Makkah as a conqueror, proclaimed a general amnesty for all but a few known criminals, most of whom were eventually forgiven. In their relief and surprise, the whole population of Makkah hastened to swear allegiance to him. The Prophet then destroyed all of the idols housed in the Ka'bah, saying: "Truth has come; falsehood has vanished," ﴾جَاءَ الْحَقُّ وَزَهَقَ الْبَاطِلُ إِنَّ الْبَاطِلَ كَانَ زَهُوقًا﴿ (17:81), and the Muslim call to prayer rang out over Makkah.

But not all tribes were so eager to embrace Islam. In that same year, an angry gathering of pagan tribes tried to regain control of the Ka'bah. The Prophet, who led twelve thousand men against them, met this new enemy at Ḥunayn. When the Muslims advanced into a deep ravine, they were ambushed and almost put to flight. With difficulty, they managed to rally to the Prophet and his bodyguard of faithful comrades who stood firm. But the victory, when it came, was complete and the booty enormous, for many of the hostile tribes had brought with them all of their possessions. The tribe of Thaqīf, which had participated in this campaign, soon saw its own city of Ṭā'if besieged and reduced to submission.

After all of this, the Prophet appointed a governor for Makkah and returned to al Madinah to the boundless joy of the Anṣār, who had feared that he might forsake them and return to his native city.

In the ninth year of the Hijrah, hearing that a new army was being assembled in Syria, the Prophet called upon the Muslims to support him in a great campaign. Many excused themselves on the grounds that the distances involved were great, that it was the hot season, that it was harvest time, and that the enemy had a great deal of prestige. Others just refused to go without offering any excuse. Both groups were denounced in the Qur'an.

﴿لَقَدْ تَابَ اللَّهُ عَلَى النَّبِيِّ وَالْمُهَاجِرِينَ وَالأَنْصَارِ الَّذِينَ اتَّبَعُوهُ فِي سَاعَةِ الْعُسْرَةِ مِنْ بَعْدِ مَا كَادَ يَزِيغُ قُلُوبُ فَرِيقٍ مِنْهُمْ ثُمَّ تَابَ عَلَيْهِمْ إِنَّهُ بِهِمْ رَءُوفٌ رَحِيمٌ(١١٧)وَعَلَى الثَّلَاثَةِ الَّذِينَ خُلِّفُوا حَتَّى إِذَا ضَاقَتْ عَلَيْهِمُ الأَرْضُ بِمَا رَحُبَتْ وَضَاقَتْ عَلَيْهِمْ أَنْفُسُهُمْ وَظَنُّوا أَنْ لاَ مَلْجَأَ مِنْ اللَّـهِ إِلاَّ إِلَيْهِ ثُمَّ تَابَ عَلَيْهِمْ لِيَتُوبُوا إِنَّ اللَّهَ هُوَ التَّوَّابُ الرَّحِيمُ﴾ (التوبة: ١١٧-١١٨).

Allah has turned in mercy to the Prophet, and to the Muhājirīn and the Anṣār who followed him in the hour of hardship. After the hearts of a party of them had almost swerved aside, then turned He unto them in mercy. Lo! He is Full of Pity, Merciful for them.

And to the three also (did He turn in mercy) who were left behind: when the earth, vast as it is, was straitened for them, and their own souls were straitened for them till they bethought them that there is no refuge from Allah save toward Him. Then turned He unto them in mercy that they (too) might turn (repentant unto Him).[8] Lo! Allah! He is the Relenting, the Merciful. (9:117–118)

The campaign ended peacefully, for the Muslims advanced to Tabūk, on the borders of Syria, and discovered that the enemy had not yet gathered.

Although Makkah had been conquered and its people were now Muslims, the official order of the pilgrimage had not been changed: the pagan Arabs performed it as usual,

---

8.   The reference is to the three men of al Madinah (Ka'b ibn Malik, Murārah ibn al Rabi', and Hilal ibn Umayyah) who were ostracized for their failing to join the Prophet's campaigns of Tabūk, but afterwards repented and were forgiven.

and the Muslims performed it in the way ordained by God. Only after the pilgrims' caravan left al Madinah in the ninth year of the Hijrah, by which time Islam was dominant in northern Arabia, was the Declaration of Disavowal revealed.

﴿يَاأَيُّهَا الَّذِينَ آمَنُوا إِنَّمَا الْمُشْرِكُونَ نَجَسٌ فَلاَ يَقْرَبُوا الْمَسْجِدَ الْحَرَامَ
بَعْدَ عَامِهِمْ هَذَا وَإِنْ خِفْتُمْ عَيْلَةً فَسَوْفَ يُغْنِيكُمُ اللَّهُ مِنْ فَضْلِهِ إِنْ شَاءَ
إِنَّ اللَّهَ عَلِيمٌ حَكِيمٌ﴾ (التوبة: ٢٨).

O you who believe! The idolaters are truly unclean. So let them not come near the Sacred Mosque after this their year. If you fear poverty (from the loss of their merchandise) Allah shall preserve you of His bounty if He will. Lo! Allah is Knower, Wise. (9:28)

The Prophet sent a copy of it by messenger to Abū Bakr, leader of the pilgrimage, with the instructions that ‘Alī was to read it to the multitudes at Makkah. In essence, it stated that after that year only Muslims and certain non-Muslims (those who had never broken their treaties with the Muslims or actively sided against them) would be allowed to make the pilgrimage. These treaties would be honored until their expiration date, after which these non-Muslims would be treated like all of the other non-Muslims. This proclamation marks the end of idol worship in Arabia.

The ninth year of the Hijrah, the Year of Deputations, saw delegations from all over Arabia coming to al Madinah to swear allegiance to the Prophet and to hear the Qur'an.[9]

---

9. *Surat al Ḥujurāt* is said to refer to the behavior of one of the deputations at a time when deputations from all parts of Arabia were coming to al Madinah to profess allegiance to the Prophet. The whole surah,

43

The Prophet had become, in fact, the ruler of Arabia, but his way of life remained as simple as before.

During the last ten years of his life, the Prophet led twenty-seven campaigns, nine of which saw heavy fighting. He planned, but let other people lead, a further thirty-eight expeditions. He personally controlled each detail of the organization, judged each case, and was accessible to each suppliant. He destroyed idolatry in Arabia, raised women from the status of chattel to human beings with complete legal equality vis-à-vis men, and ended the drunkenness and immorality that had until his time disgraced the Arabs. His followers fell in love with faith, sincerity, and honest dealing. Previously ignorant tribes who had been content with their ignorance were transformed into tribes with a great thirst for knowledge. And, for the first time in history, the ideal of universal human brotherhood was a fact and a principle of common law. The Prophet's support and guide in all of this work was the Qur'an.

In the tenth year of the Hijrah, the Prophet performed the pilgrimage to Makkah for the last time. This has become known as the Farewell Pilgrimage. From Mount 'Arafat, he preached to an enormous throng of pilgrims, reminded them of the duties enjoined upon them by God, and that one day they would meet and be judged by their Lord on the basis of what they had done here on Earth. At the end of the discourse, he asked: "Have I conveyed the message?" And from that great multitude of people, who a few months or years before had all been conscienceless idolaters, the shout

---

dealing as it does with manners and particularly with behavior toward the Prophet, evidently belongs to a period when there were many people seeking an audience, many of whom were quite uncivilized.

went up: "O Allah! Yes!" The Prophet said: "O Allah! You are a witness!"

It was during this Farewell Pilgrimage that *Surat al Naṣr* (Succour), which he received as an announcement of his approaching death, was revealed. Soon after his return to al Madinah he fell ill, an event that caused dismay throughout Arabia and anguish to the people of al Madinah, Makkah, and Ṭā'if. In the early dawn on his last day of earthly life, he came out of his room beside the mosque at al Madinah and joined the public prayer, which Abū Bakr had been leading since his illness. This event caused a great relief among the people, who took this as an indication that he was well again.

When later in the day the rumour spread that he had died, 'Umar declared it a crime to think that the Prophet could die and threatened to punish severely anyone who said such a thing. Abū Bakr, upon entering the mosque and seeing what 'Umar was doing, went to 'Ā'ishah's (his daughter's) chamber to see the Prophet. Ascertaining that the Prophet really was dead, he kissed the Prophet's forehead, returned to the mosque, and tried to whisper the information to 'Umar, who was still threatening the people. Finally, because 'Umar refused to listen to him, Abū Bakr called out to the people. Recognizing his voice, they left 'Umar and turned their attention to Abū Bakr who, after praising God, said: "O people! As for him who used to worship Muhammad, Muhammad is dead. But as for him who used to worship Allah, Allah is alive and does not die." He then recited the following verse:

45

﴿وَمَا مُحَمَّدٌ إِلاَّ رَسُولٌ قَدْ خَلَتْ مِنْ قَبْلِهِ الرُّسُلُ أَفَإِنْ مَاتَ أَوْ قُتِلَ انْقَلَبْتُمْ عَلَى أَعْقَابِكُمْ وَمَنْ يَنْقَلِبْ عَلَى عَقِبَيْهِ فَلَنْ يَضُرَّ اللَّهَ شَيْئًا وَسَيَجْزِي اللَّهُ الشَّاكِرِينَ﴾ (آل عمران: ١٤٤).

And Muhammad is but a Messenger, messengers the like of whom have passed away before him. Will it be that, when he dies or is slain, you will turn back on your heels? He who turns back does no hurt to Allah and Allah will reward the thankful. (3:144)

"And," says the narrator, an eyewitness, "it was as if the people had not known that such a verse had been revealed until Abū Bakr recited it." Another witness tells how 'Umar used to say: "As soon as I heard Abū Bakr recite that verse, my feet were cut from beneath me and I fell to the ground, for I knew that Allah's Messenger was dead. May Allah bless and keep him!"

ADDENDUM:

AL QUR'AN

All the surahs of the Qur'an had been recorded in writing before the Prophet's death, and many Muslims had committed the whole Qur'an to memory. But the written surahs were dispersed among the people. This soon became a problem, for within two years of the Prophet's death, many of those who had memorized the entire Qur'an were killed during a battle. It was therefore decided to collect the written portions and prepare a complete and undeniably authentic written copy of the Qur'an. All existing copies were collected during the reign of 'Uthmān, and an authoritative version based on Abū Bakr's collection and the testimony of those who could recite the entire Qur'an from memory was compiled. This is the Qur'an that exists today, which is regarded as traditional and as being arranged according to the Prophet's own instructions. The caliph 'Uthmān and his helpers, all Companions of the Prophet and the most devout students of the revelation, saw that this task was completed. The Qur'an has thus been very carefully preserved.

The arrangement is not easy to understand. Revelations of various dates and on different subjects are found together; verses revealed in al Madinah are found in Makkan surahs; some Madinan surahs that were revealed quite late are found in the front of the Qur'an while the very early Makkan surahs come at the end. This arrangement is not haphazard, however, as some have hastily supposed. Closer study reveals a sequence and significance, for instance, with regard to placing the very early Makkan surahs at the end. The inspiration of the Prophet progressed from the internal to the external, whereas most people find their way through the external to the internal.

Another disconcerting peculiarity proceeds from one of the beauties of the original and is unavoidable without abolishing the division of the verses, which is of great importance for reference. In Arabic, verses are divided according to the rhythm of the language. When a certain sound marking the rhythm recurs, there is a strong pause and the verse ends naturally, although the sentence may go on to the next verse or to several subsequent verses. This is the spirit of the Arabic language. Unfortunately, attempts to reproduce such rhythm in English have the opposite effect. Here only the division is preserved, the verses being divided as in the Qur'an, and numbered.